EXTREME ABILITIES

AMAZING HUMAN FEATS
AND THE SIMPLE SCIENCE BEHIND THEM

WRITTEN BY **GALADRIEL WATSON**
ILLUSTRATED BY **CORNELIA LI**

annick press
toronto + berkeley

Cover art/design by Cornelia Li/Danielle Arbour
Edited by Linda Pruessen
Designed by Danielle Arbour

Annick Press Ltd.

We acknowledge the support of the Canada Council for the Arts and the Ontario Arts Council, and the participation of the Government of Canada/la participation du gouvernement du Canada for our publishing activities.

Cataloging in Publication

Watson, Galadriel, author
    Extreme abilities : amazing human feats and the simple science behind them / Galadriel Watson ; Cornelia Li, illustrator.
Issued in print and electronic formats.
ISBN 978-1-77321-250-0 (hardcover).--ISBN 978-1-77321-249-4 (softcover).--ISBN 978-1-77321-252-4 (HTML).--ISBN 978-1-77321-251-7 (PDF)
    1. Human body--Miscellanea--Juvenile literature. 2. Curiosities and wonders--Juvenile literature. 3. Ability--Miscellanea--Juvenile literature.
I. Title.
QP37.W375 2018   j612   C2018-904331-8
                                                     C2018-904332-6

Published in the U.S.A. by Annick Press (U.S.) Ltd.
Distributed in Canada by University of Toronto Press.
Distributed in the U.S.A. by Publishers Group West.

Printed in China

annickpress.com
galadrielwatson.com
corneliali.com

Also available as an e-book. Please visit www.annickpress.com/ebooks.html for more details.

CONTENTS

TAKING IT *to the* MAX

Over 200 bones. About 640 muscles. Roughly 86 billion brain cells. Your body is complicated, sophisticated, and fascinating. Everything you do—from lifting a spoonful of cereal to your mouth to writing a test—requires many body parts to communicate and coordinate.

For your entire life, your body has been achieving wondrous things. You began balancing on two feet—and then maybe on two wheels. You started counting blocks—and then adding numbers. Every day, your body is using all those parts, from bones to brain, while adapting and learning new skills. And sometimes—just sometimes—the skills go beyond the norm …

In your case, maybe you can cross your eyes or curl your tongue. Maybe you're fantastic at cartwheeling or Hula-Hooping. Maybe you can easily remember tons of weird facts.

The people you'll meet in this book can do amazing things too—even more than amazing—things so extreme, in fact, they might seem impossible. How about hoisting a horse? Walking around the world? Solving tough math problems in mere seconds?

These people will astound you, and their feats may seem magical. But almost all of these amazing achievements can be explained by science—the science of the human body. As we get to know these men and women, we'll explore how their bodies and brains work together to make the seemingly impossible possible. We'll also take a peek at the risks behind these activities—and there are plenty! It's important to remember that the people in this book either were born with these traits or trained long and hard to get them. Never put yourself in danger by trying to copy what they've done.

While we'll tell you some ways you can safely improve your skills in these areas, always respect your own limits. Go slowly, listen to your body, and talk to an adult before pushing yourself. By proceeding at your personal pace, you too might someday have abilities worth bragging about.

Now let's see the crazy things people can do! 👉

Chapter 1

MASTERS of MUSCLE

Every seat in the auditorium is filled. More people line the walls, and hundreds of others have been turned away at the door. But despite the crowd, the space is quiet.

It's May 27, 1895. The audience in Boston, Massachusetts, is frozen with anticipation. All eyes are on the man on the stage. Louis Cyr, born in Quebec, Canada, is already famous for his strength, but now he's going to prove without a doubt he's the strongest man of all.

Louis picks 18 men out of the audience, the biggest ones he can find. The men are weighed. They step together onto a platform resting on wooden supports.

Louis bends. He slips under the platform. He rests the top of his back against it. His goal: to lift all 1,967 kilograms (4,336 pounds). Yesterday's newspaper declared in huge letters: "CYR PROMISES A BIG SENSATION TOMORROW MORNING AT 10:50." But can Louis do it?

He heaves. His muscles strain. His legs push. His face turns red. The platform starts to tremble. The platform starts to lift. Finally, it clears the supports. The audience erupts in cheers.

PUMP IT!

Lifting 18 men was just one of Louis Cyr's incredible feats. As a teen, he lifted a large horse off the ground. A decade later, he resisted the pull of four horses—two hitched to each of his arms. Some people have called him "the Strongest Man Who Ever Lived," even though lots of other old-time strongmen were also impressing audiences around the world. With stage names like "the French Hercules" and "the Cannonball King," they were tons of fun to watch.

Today, people continue to astound us with seemingly superhuman strength. Follow the World's Strongest Man contest, which has been running for more than 40 years, and you'll see men hauling two refrigerators at once, flipping huge poles, throwing heavy kegs over a wall, lifting boulders, and more. And check out Canadian Kevin Fast. In 2013, he managed to hike 11 people up on his shoulders, the platform on which they were standing swaying like a raft at sea. The total weight: 777.9 kilograms (1,715 pounds). Not Louis's record, but still mighty impressive.

Women have also racked up some jaw-dropping achievements. In the 1940s—a time when few women lifted weights—Abbye "Pudgy" Stockton had no pudge on her: she was all muscle. Living in Los Angeles, California, and known as "the Queen of Muscle Beach," she could lift her husband above her head.

Then there's Varya Akulova. Born in Ukraine in 1992, Varya could carry her father on her back by age seven and was already winning weightlifting events. She's been called "the Strongest Girl in the World," while Richard Sandrak, also born in 1992 in Ukraine, has been dubbed "the World's Strongest Boy." Richard could lift three times his own body weight when he was still a kid.

TEENAGER LIFTS CAR

In 2013, American sisters Haylee and Hannah Smith, aged 14 and 16, lifted a tractor off their father after it flipped over and trapped him. In 2015, 19-year-old Charlotte Heffelmire, also from the States, lifted a truck after a jack collapsed, pinning her father under it.

How did these regular folks, under extreme pressure, develop a temporary strength they never knew they had?

First, the stories are often exaggerated. When someone claims to have lifted a vehicle, they probably lifted only one corner. Three tires remained on the ground, greatly reducing the weight. (Think of your living room couch. All by yourself, you probably can't pick up the whole thing. But try lifting only one corner and you might find success.)

Second, in scary situations, epinephrine (also known as adrenaline) rushes into our blood. This hormone helps us react to "fight or flight" situations, when we have to decide whether to fight something (such as a bear) or run away. Our hearts beat faster and we breathe faster. More oxygen goes to our brains, making us more alert. Additional nutrients flood into our bloodstreams. Although our muscles don't suddenly get as strong as a superhero's, "fight or flight" effects can take the abilities we've got and give them a slightly more powerful push.

HOW IT'S DONE!

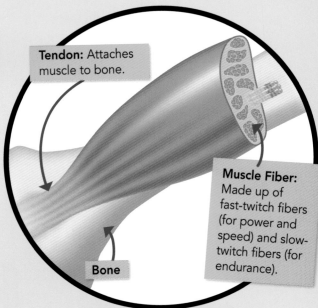

Tendon: Attaches muscle to bone.

Muscle Fiber: Made up of fast-twitch fibers (for power and speed) and slow-twitch fibers (for endurance).

Bone

Where does strength—nearly superhuman or just plain human—come from?

For the most part, it comes from our muscles, which are activated by the brain and the rest of the central nervous system. Together, these form the neuromuscular system, which produces movement.

Our muscles are made of millions of tightly packed fibers. When you do an activity that stresses the muscle—like lifting weights—these fibers get damaged. They repair themselves while you rest, getting bigger so they can handle the stress better the next time.

Not all people who stress their muscles will get bulky and mind-blowingly strong, though. Each person has different quantities and types of fibers, and your muscles probably won't grow enough to enable you to lift a fridge.

Your muscles are made up of two types of fibers. Slow-twitch fibers are used for endurance sports, such as long-distance running. Fast-twitch fibers are powerful and used for quick, explosive movements, such as hauling a huge barbell over your head. Your body—and each muscle—has its own combination of these two types. This means you might be born to be a sprinter, or maybe you're more of a natural at carrying a platform of people on your shoulders. Although you can train to make your slow-twitch fibers stronger and your fast-twitch fibers last longer, you pretty much keep the fibers you've got.

FAST FACT
Toss Me That Straw
Scotland's Highland Games is one of the oldest competitions for strongmen. Introduced in the year 1040, they helped the king decide which men would make the best soldiers. These days, the contestants still vie to toss stones, throw hammers, and lob bundles of straw with a pitchfork.

STOP THAT!

Your body is filled with chalones. No, these aren't a yummy Mexican meal. They're substances found in the cells of our tissues that regulate their growth.

In the case of our muscles, the main chalone is a protein called myostatin. As our bodies grow, our muscles grow too. Once these muscles get to their proper adult size, there's enough myostatin in them to kick into action. Its job: to tell the muscles to stop getting bigger.

Sometimes, something turns out differently. In the early 2000s, researchers studied one child who lacked myostatin. Even as a baby, he was super muscly. By age four and a half, he could hold a 3-kilogram (6.6-pound) dumbbell in each hand and lift his arms out to the sides. This also may be how other young children can wow us with their age-defying strength. And was it Louis Cyr's secret too? No one knows.

Researchers are now working on how to use myostatin to our advantage—not necessarily to create extra-powerful humans, but to treat diseases like muscular dystrophy that waste away patients' muscles. So far, they've been able to block myostatin in mice and macaques to give them bigger and stronger muscles. But they haven't yet tried it on humans.

HAZARD ALERT!

Even if their muscles are packed with the right kind of fast-twitch fibers, people who lift too much weight too quickly may strain or tear their muscles, especially in areas like the shoulders or lower back. And we're not talking about the tiny kinds of damage that help the muscles get stronger, but the bigger kinds that mean something's gone wrong. Extreme lifters can also tear their tendons—the tissues that connect muscles to bone—thanks to lifting heavy weights up and down, up and down, again and again.

OVER TO YOU

In general, though, weight training is good for you. It can improve your health by lowering your blood pressure. You may sleep more soundly. You may have higher self-esteem as it helps you feel better about your body and its abilities. Since using muscles demands so much energy, training burns calories and helps keep your body lean. If you play other sports, it can help you perform better. And not only will your muscles get stronger, but the good strain on your skeleton helps strengthen your bones.

Even children as young as seven can use light weights. But no matter your age, make sure you get the okay from a doctor before starting. Work with a certified trainer to develop a training

program and learn proper technique—you might hurt yourself if you try to figure out how to use the equipment yourself. Have someone supervise while you work out. Remember to rest between workouts: this is when your muscles repair and get stronger.

Oh yeah, and make sure to think of a great stage name. One day, you might need it!

FAST **FACT**

As Strong as a Viking

Legend says that 1,000 years ago, a Viking named Orm Storolfsson hoisted the mast of his ship—that's the pole that holds up the sails—onto his shoulders and shuffled a few feet forward. In 2015, Iceland's Hafthór Júlíus Björnsson reenacted this feat, lifting a log onto his back and taking five whole steps. Orm had only managed three!

Chapter 2

PRETZEL PEOPLE

In a black-lace, skin-tight bodysuit, the woman known as "Zlata" enters the blue-lit stage. She places her feet on two small raised platforms. On the floor between the platforms sits a vase of flowers. Zlata's goal? To bend down, pick up one flower at a time with her teeth, straighten up, and release the flower into a second vase set at face-level.

Sounds like a challenge, but not impossible, right? Here's the twist: Zlata isn't bending forward to fetch each flower, but *backward*. By stretching her stomach and scrunching her spine, she's able to arch back and then return to an upright position, again and again—enough to pick up six flowers in one minute and earn a 2014 Guinness World Record. Later she beat her own record and picked up eleven.

Oh, and she can also squeeze herself into a box the size of a carry-on suitcase. Bizarre, right?

Born in Russia in 1984, Zlata calls herself "the Goddess of Flexibility" (her real name is Julia Günthel). At age four, she realized she was more flexible than most girls in her class. At eight, she started studying circus skills. By ten, she was a professional contortionist.

What's a contortionist? Someone who can squish, stretch, or twist in amazing ways.

STRETCHY SHOWTIME

Contortionists have been around for thousands of years. In medieval times, they often appeared at fairgrounds. These days, they stun audiences in circuses, perform stunts in movies, or strut their super-flexible stuff at sports halftime shows.

FAST FACT
The Incredible Shrinking Student
School is supposed to expand your mind—but is it also restricting your body? One study showed that at age five, almost all kids could touch their toes. By age twelve, only 30 percent could. Some researchers speculate that all those hours sitting at school could be the cause.

Many are flexible in only one way: they're great at bending forward or at bending backward. Some, like Zlata, are impressive in both directions. Others can dislocate their arms or legs, or even turn their torsos to face their rears, like the American Daniel Browning Smith, who calls himself "Rubberboy." Some can turn their heads far enough to look right behind themselves, like Germany's Martin Laurello, who performed from the 1920s to the 1940s as "the Human Owl." Nowadays, an American clown and circus performer called "Scarlet Checkers" challenges audience members to pick two body parts they think she won't be able to touch together. So far, she's always won the game.

A WIDE RANGE of ABILITIES

How old are you? What gender are you? Your answers are clues to your flexibility.

Maybe you were flexible when you were little—most of us start out with great range of motion, but we get stiffer as we get older. Also, females are generally more flexible than males, and pregnant women are even *more* flexible, thanks to hormones like relaxin. Relaxin loosens the ligaments and realigns collagen fibers in the pelvic area, making childbirth easier.

Studies have also shown that many people of African, Asian, and Middle Eastern descent are born more flexible than others. This is probably because of a particular collagen structure they've inherited.

FAST FACT

I Confess!

To some people, stretching feels like torture—and once upon a time, it was. From ancient Greece to medieval Europe, people used machines like the rack or a team of horses to stretch people limb to limb, either to force a confession or to punish them for their crimes.

HOW IT'S DONE!

Several factors affect flexibility.

First, our joints—the points in our bodies at which two bones meet—allow for only so much movement. It's all dependent on the shapes of the bones and the sockets or notches they fit into. Then there are the ligaments, the cords that attach bone to bone; these are pretty rigid and don't stretch much. Our muscle fibers, though, are pretty stretchy. However, these fibers are bundled together by tighter connective tissues, and the muscles are attached to bones via tight cords called tendons.

To increase flexibility, it's the muscles and their connective tissues we generally work on. Over time, stretching allows them to loosen and adjust to new lengths.

So, have people like Scarlet Checkers and Zlata simply stretched and stretched until they can do what they can do?

In some cases. But many contortionists are hypermobile (meaning they're flexible beyond what's normal) because of a group of conditions called Ehlers-Danlos syndrome (EDS). Doctors have discovered

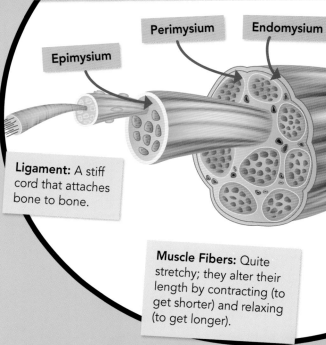

The tight connective tissues that bind the muscles together; they can become stretchier with training.

Perimysium

Endomysium

Epimysium

Ligament: A stiff cord that attaches bone to bone.

Muscle Fibers: Quite stretchy; they alter their length by contracting (to get shorter) and relaxing (to get longer).

that Zlata has EDS, as do Scarlet Checkers and Rubberboy.

Ligaments, tendons, and other connective tissues are made up of proteins called elastin and collagen. As you can guess by the name, elastin is elastic, meaning it can stretch like a rubber band. Collagen is very stiff. Some connective tissues are mostly made of collagen, making them less flexible (think ligament). Others have more elastin mixed in with the collagen, making them easier to stretch (like

Bone and Socket: Allows for only so much range of motion.

Tendon: A stiff cord that attaches muscle to bone.

the tissues that wrap around our muscles). Also, some people are born with greater proportions of elastin, meaning they're naturally more flexible.

The issue for people with EDS, though, isn't their elastin. It's about the quality of their collagen. Because of an unusual structure, which was probably inherited from their parents, their collagen is too elastic. This means they can move their bodies in ways the rest of us can't.

FAST **FACT**

A Long-Term Liability
Dancers need to be flexible to excel at their art—but not too flexible. While many young dance students show signs of extreme flexibility, not as many long-term professionals do. Researchers think this may be because dancers with extreme flexibility get injured more often, take longer to heal, and are forced to leave the dance world sooner—or maybe they learn to control their muscles and become more stable.

OVER TO YOU

But what if you don't have EDS? Can you become more flexible too?

You bet, and persistence is key. Stretch slowly and with control. Never push yourself. If a particular stretch doesn't feel right, back out of it. The safest way to increase your flexibility is to gently enter a position that challenges your current limit and hold it.

Sometimes, a more dynamic method of stretching can warm you up for a sport, such as when a baseball player swings a weighted bat or a dancer tosses her leg back and forth. However, these vigorous movements are more likely to injure you.

There's also a method called "proprioceptive neuromuscular

facilitation." Huh? This big term means that you alternate between stretching a muscle and flexing it. When a muscle is stretched, the body fears an injury is about to happen. Going into defensive mode, it causes the muscle to contract, or flex. This is called the "myotatic stretch reflex." By flexing the muscle on purpose, you're essentially telling your body you're in control and it doesn't need to use this reflex. Then when you stretch again, the muscle is able to relax a bit further. But save this method until you're older, and learn how to do it properly—it too can cause injury.

We all need to be flexible—to a certain degree. We need a decent range of motion to perform our everyday tasks and do the sports we love.

If we're sore or injured, stretching can relieve discomfort and help us heal by sending more blood and oxygen to the area. People in activities like gymnastics, figure skating, and dance need to push their flexibility even further. Even hockey players need to be flexible—think of those goaltender splits!

With time and careful practice, your body will gradually expand its limits. You may never be able to backbend to pick up flowers, but then again, do you really want to?

FAST FACT

The Demon Violinist

Niccolò Paganini, born in what we now call Italy in 1782, was such an astounding violinist that some people thought he was possessed by the devil. What he was really possessed by, though, could have been Ehlers-Danlos syndrome. While researchers can't know for sure, they say this is the most likely reason he could stretch his fingers so far and wow his audiences.

AMAZING MONGOLIA

Not so long ago, circus skills like contortionism were passed down through families or from teacher to apprentice. These days, there are circus schools dedicated to all sorts of stunts, including extreme flexibility. These include San Francisco's Circus Center and the École nationale de cirque in Montreal.

But many of the best contortionists come from Mongolia. Squeezed between China and Russia, this country considers contortionism a national tradition. People there have been practicing the art for hundreds of years, perhaps because they've inherited traits that make them good at it. In the 1940s, Mongolian contortionists began seriously training so they could perform in the new State Circus.

In North America or, say, Russia, children may dream of one day dancing ballet; in Mongolia, they often dream of becoming contortionists. Now, these practitioners are working in many other countries, including with Canada's famous Cirque du Soleil. They're also spreading their intense training methods (at least 15 hours a week) to the world.

Chapter 3

MIND~BOGGLING MEMORIZERS

Most of the time, Jake Hausler is a normal 11-year-old kid. He likes to play soccer and baseball with his friends. He likes to cheer on the baseball and hockey teams in his hometown of St. Louis, Missouri. Today, though, he sits in a research lab. A mass of black-coated wires snakes from his head, secured on to him like a hat. The cords are measuring what's going on in his brain.

"What happened on April 8, 2013?" the researcher asks, referring to a date a couple of years back.

Jake immediately answers. "I went to the St. Louis Zoo."

For Jake, this quick response isn't unusual. If you ask him about any day over the past several years, he'll know what he was doing. He knows what date he watched the seventh game of baseball's 2011 World Series. He knows that the St. Louis Cardinals beat the Texas Rangers, 6–2, and he knows who pitched for both teams. He knows exactly what date and day of the week he saw *Iron Man 3*, years ago.

Most of us can remember whether we had toast or cereal for breakfast this morning, what color shirt we wore yesterday, and maybe if it rained last Wednesday. But over time, we remember only the big stuff—things like a great camping trip or taking a bad spill off a bike.

Jake, on the other hand, remembers a heck of a lot more.

MEMORY MAGIC

Jake has what's called a Highly Superior Autobiographical Memory (HSAM). People with HSAM compare their memories to time travel: give them a date from any time since they were small children—even if it was decades ago—and it's as if they were back there. They can remember the major events of the day, relive the big emotions, and maybe even smell the smells and feel their clothes.

Other people have a different kind of memory skill. How about memorizing 10 license plate numbers in one minute? Or taking two minutes to memorize the order of a deck of shuffled playing cards? Or spending an hour to memorize 1,000 random numbers?

That's what "memory athletes" do at events like the USA Memory Challenge or the World Memory Championships. And some of these athletes are young. India's Sri Vyshnavi Yarlagadda has been traveling to memory competitions since she was fifteen and has won fistfuls of medals. A German boy named Konstantin Skudler won the World Memory Championship Children's Competition when he was only nine.

FAST FACT

Remember Like the Romans

If we can't remember a fact, we google it. But back in ancient Rome, people like politicians and lawyers, who needed to have important information on the tips of their tongues, would train slaves to remember the facts for them.

A BIG PIECE OF PI

Homework and to-do lists aren't the only things you can memorize. Some memory whizzes focus on gigantic pieces of pi—no, not apple pie! In geometry, pi is a number that equals the distance around a circle divided by the distance across. It's usually shortened to 3.14, but the number actually goes on forever. In 2006, a man named Akira Haraguchi recounted 100,000 digits from memory, which took him over 16 hours.

To memorize pi, you can use "pi writing" or "Pilish." You write a story, choosing words with the number of letters that match the digits you want to memorize. For example, to remember the first seven digits—3.141592—you could say, "How I wish I could calculate pi."

If you're not keen on pi, how about literature? A man named John Basinger spent an hour a day over nine years to memorize the 60,000-word poem *Paradise Lost* by John Milton. That's like memorizing over three-quarters of the first Harry Potter book!

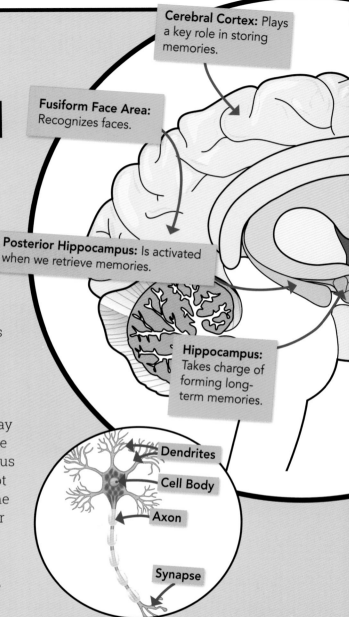

Cerebral Cortex: Plays a key role in storing memories.

Fusiform Face Area: Recognizes faces.

Posterior Hippocampus: Is activated when we retrieve memories.

Hippocampus: Takes charge of forming long-term memories.

Dendrites

Cell Body

Axon

Synapse

Here's how memory works:

When you experience an event or come across a fact you wish to remember, the information is sent to the part of your brain called the hippocampus. The hippocampus processes the information and interacts with the cerebral cortex to store it. If the event was unremarkable, like a bird flying past the window, the memory probably won't last. But if the event was fairly emotional, like a super-fun birthday party, another part of the brain called the amygdala will influence the hippocampus to make the memory strong. If you've got an upcoming test at school, repeating the facts a lot helps make them solid in your memory too.

Different kinds of memories aren't kept all in one place. The memory of how the birthday cake looked, for example, is stored in the brain cells (neurons) in one area of the brain, while the taste of the chocolate icing is stored in another. When it's time to remember the memory, your brain's frontal lobe sends out an electrical command. This makes the various areas of your brain retrieve the memories to present you with one big picture.

Can you train your brain to remember daily life as well as people like Jake? Researchers say no. People with HSAM are born able to keep their memories longer and retrieve them faster than usual, and researchers know of fewer than 100 people who have it. Tests on

Frontal Lobe: Starts the remembering process.

Caudate Nucleus: Stores information about actions we perform without thinking (like how to ride a bike) and is somewhat larger in HSAMs.

Amygdala: Is activated by strong emotions and influences the creation of strong memories, like flashbulb memories, in other brain regions.

Temporal Lobe: Stores info like facts and dates and is significantly larger in HSAMs—and elephants!

Before you launch into rewiring your brain, remember that forgetting things is actually a healthy part of memory. It shows that your brain is holding on to what's important and letting go of what's not.

And although an astonishing memory like Jake's sounds great, it may be good that you can't remember everything you've done. Some people with HSAM say they have a hard time focusing on the present when their brains are always replaying the past. And imagine reliving your worst day or most embarrassing moment over and over—in detail.

Still, memorizing can be both fun and useful. You may get frustrated, but try different methods and take it easy on yourself. Most memory athletes limit their daily practice to half an hour or less. So turn off Netflix and take the time to exercise your brain instead!

their brains have shown that two areas are bigger than average. But researchers don't yet know if these areas differ *because* these people have HSAM or if the differences are what cause HSAM.

But you might be able to become a memory athlete. One study showed that practicing for just 3 minutes a day for 40 days helped non-athletes vastly improve their memory skills. Researchers also discovered that while memory athletes' brains are structured just like anyone else's, this training affects how connections form in their brains.

FAST FACT

What's Your Best Friend's Phone Number?

Not so long ago, people had to memorize phone numbers and other simple facts. Now we don't bother, since this information is just a click away. Researchers consider this a type of "transactive memory," in which we rely on an outside source to hold the facts for us. It's just like asking your mother what time tonight's movie is playing at the theater: instead of remembering the time yourself, you're relying on her to do it for you.

OVER TO YOU

Here's the trick: The best way to remember a fact is to turn it into a vivid mental picture. The more vivid you make the picture, the more connections it will make in your brain and the easier it will be to remember. And the more often you practice memorizing in this way, the better you'll get at it.

One of the most popular and effective ways of remembering is to create a "memory palace." Picture a place you know well in real life, like your house. To remember things, envision placing them inside.

Really use your imagination to make your memory stand out by picturing something a bit bizarre. For example, if you have to remember to bring a permission slip to school, you can leave it loudly flapping around the front door, like a bird. If you have to remember to talk to your art teacher, you can imagine her in the kitchen, madly mixing colorful paints into wonderful-smelling cupcakes. Once you get to school, all you have to do is mentally walk through your palace and these things will jump out of your memory.

FAST FACT

Do Plants Have Memories?

It looks like they do. Researchers trained garden pea seedlings to grow toward a fan by teaching them that behind the fan was a nourishing light. How did the plants remember that a breeze from a fan meant a light would come next? Researchers don't yet know.

Memorization methods like this are called "mnemonics." Here's another one: to remember lists, you can create weird sentences, rhymes, or simple words. For example:

• My Very Excellent Mother Just Served Us Nachos stands for the order of our solar system's eight planets.

• HOMES stands for the Great Lakes: Huron, Ontario, Michigan, Erie, Superior.

And turning a list into a song is how most of us learned our ABCs!

Even if you're not planning to match wits with world champions, strengthening your memory muscles can be fun and build confidence. The next time you've got a school test, how about putting a technique or two into action? Store your math formulas in a memory palace, create a rhyme for historical events, or belt out French words in song—just remember to sing them silently in your head at test time!

UNFORGETTABLE

Many types of memories come naturally. Some of these we all might experience sooner or later in our lives. Others, like HSAM, are much more extraordinary.

• Have you ever attended an amazing event, like a huge Christmas parade? Or witnessed something awful, like a car crash? If so, you may remember it well into the future. These are called "flashbulb memories," and the strong emotions you felt influenced your amygdala and hippocampus to sear them into your brain.

• Some children have what's called "eidetic memories." These kids can look at a picture for 30 seconds, look away, and then describe it in great detail. After a few minutes, the memory fades. This enhanced ability probably means their brains haven't developed the usual memory-making capabilities yet. As they grow up and their brains mature, these kids lose this skill.

• "Super-recognizers" are better than average at recognizing and remembering faces, even after seeing a face only once, possibly many years ago. Police departments use them to look at video footage of crimes to help identify criminals.

• People called "savants" may be able to memorize an encyclopedia or know thousands of songs by heart. Most savants also have the brain condition called autism, although scientists aren't sure why.

Chapter 4

ULTRA~LONG EXPERTS

Headlamps illuminating the dark of night. Rain plummeting off the tips of noses. Mountainsides soggy with snow. Muddy footprints marking the way. Wind whipping sleet sideways. Rocky trails and scraped knees.

Britain's Lizzy Hawker and 2,300 other racers plow through a miserable night in the Alps. While most other people were eating dinner, they set off from Chamonix, France, to run the 2012 edition of the Ultra-Trail du Mont Blanc (UTMB), one of the toughest endurance races in the world. The weather has been so bad that this year's route has been shortened: only 104 kilometers (65 miles) instead of the usual 171 kilometers (106 miles). But shorter doesn't mean easier.

Step by step. Moment by moment. That's how Lizzy encourages herself to continue. Eventually, dawn rises, although the sky remains thick gray. Spectators line the route, ringing cowbells and yelling encouragements. Holding strong, Lizzy slaps hands with people in the crowd as she passes. She powers toward the finish line. Closer, closer, closer—yes! With a time of 12 hours and 32 minutes, Lizzy has won the women's top spot!

Not only that, but she has also become the only person—woman or man—to win this hardest of races five times. No wonder her smile is wide.

GIVIN' IT

Longest. Wettest. Coldest. Hottest. Hardest. When it comes to athletic events that test human endurance, there are tons of options.

If you sign up for the Badwater Ultramarathon, you start in California's Death Valley. The road gets so hot that racers have to run on the painted white lines or the soles of their shoes may melt. From there—the lowest point in North America—they climb up, up, up for 217 kilometers (135 miles). They finish (or not) on the side of Mount Whitney. If you were driving at highway speeds, this trek might take you about two hours. For the parched, sleep-deprived runners, it usually takes about forty.

Speaking of sleep-deprived, how do you think you would feel after biking all the way across the United States? In the Race Across America, cyclists zoom down highways for up to 12 days, hardly taking time to rest. The goal: to cross from the Pacific Ocean in California to the Atlantic Ocean in Maryland. It's so nonstop, some racers have fallen asleep while riding!

If you prefer water, all the world's waterways are open to you. In 2014, Australian Chloe McCardel took 41.5 hours to swim between two islands in the Bahamas. In 2009, Slovenia's Martin Strel, known as "the Fish Man," took 66 days to swim down South America's Amazon River.

Or why not combine all three activities in a triathlon like the Ironman World Championship in Hawaii? You'll be swimming with sharks, biking over lava fields, and running on already-wobbly legs.

WILD, SANDY, AND LONG

If the Badwater Ultramarathon sounds like your cup of tea, here are a couple more options.

For the Barkley Marathons, all you have to do is run five loops of the 32-kilometer (20-mile) course, and you have a whole 60 hours to do it. Sounds easy—but those loops send you through the steep, thorny, muddy Tennessee wilds, with few set trails. Hardly anyone manages to slog it past three loops.

Or how about the Marathon des Sables? In French, *sable* means sand. You guessed it: this race takes place in a desert. Morocco's Sahara Desert, to be specific, where runners take six days—carrying all the food and supplies they need on their backs—to race about 254 kilometers (158 miles). The ever-changing course is kept secret until just before the event, so runners can't cheat and stash supplies. They may even get lost in sandstorms.

For a slower pace—but longer distance—plan to walk around the entire world. While the circumference of Earth at the equator is 40,075 kilometers (24,901 miles), having oceans in the way means your walk is actually much shorter, and you can rest while you take a plane or boat across the watery parts. The first person recorded to walk around the world by himself was America's Dave Kunst, who started his four-year, 23,255-kilometer (14,450-mile) trek in 1970.

HOW IT'S DONE!

Endurance athletes may have muscular arms for swimming or bulked-up legs for biking—thanks to hard training and lots of those long-lasting slow-twitch muscle fibers. But when it comes to long-distance running, there's a reason humans are particularly great: we've been doing it for about two million years.

That's when our ancestors started eating meat. Back then, they hadn't invented tools and were much too small to fight a creature like a saber-toothed cat and win. Instead, their technique was to chase the animal until it was too hot and exhausted to run anymore—and then it was easier to kill. This is called "persistence hunting" and is still used by some cultures today, including the San in

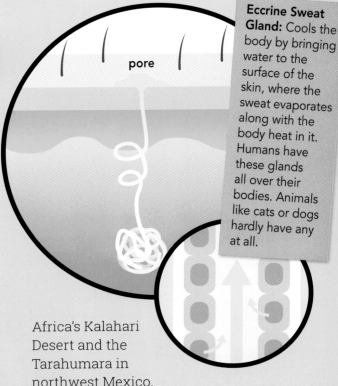

pore

Eccrine Sweat Gland: Cools the body by bringing water to the surface of the skin, where the sweat evaporates along with the body heat in it. Humans have these glands all over their bodies. Animals like cats or dogs hardly have any at all.

Africa's Kalahari Desert and the Tarahumara in northwest Mexico.

Sure, lots of animals are faster than humans. After all, they have four legs instead of two. But when it comes to running long distances, humans are the best. While we have springlike feet and legs, and strong rear-end muscles that power us forward, our top advantage is probably our ability to dissipate heat.

On a scorching summer day, you may have noticed how dogs pant—that's their way of lowering their body temperature. Well, humans have a better way: we sweat. Without fur and with tons of sweat glands, we can release heat through our skin. This helps our bodies stay cool enough to carry on—long after the saber-toothed cat has given up.

FAST FACT
The Original Race
The running race known as a marathon is just over 42 kilometers (26 miles) long, and an "ultramarathon" is any race longer than that. In 490 BCE, a runner named Pheidippides ran from the battlefield at Marathon, Greece, to the city of Athens to bring the good news that the Greeks had won against Persia. The distance was—you guessed it— about 42 kilometers (26 miles).

HAZARD ALERT!

Of course, endurance athletes can only push so hard. Too much pounding the pavement can cause stress fractures in their bones. Their hearts and other muscles can get overworked too. In super-hot weather, athletes can overheat. They can drink too little and get dehydrated. But drinking too much water can be life-threatening too, as it lowers the balance of sodium in the body and causes cells to swell—if this happens in the brain, it can be fatal.

Athletes can even see things that aren't there, from bright-green lizards to low-flying airplanes. These hallucinations often occur during overnight races, when it's dark and there are creepy shadows. But researchers suspect the main reason is that the athletes have had little or no chance to sleep—and lack of sleep can affect how we think.

Being in water may present other challenges. Athletes can suffer in ice-cold conditions. They could be stung by jellyfish or bitten by piranhas. While navigating the Amazon River, Martin Strel had to dodge drug runners and pirates.

FAST FACT

It's a Bird!

Tiny birds called Arctic terns can travel astonishing distances—nearly 96,560 kilometers (60,000 miles) per year. Over a 30-year life span, that's like traveling to the moon and back four times. For the longest nonstop flight, look to the bar-tailed godwit. Without stopping to sleep, eat, or drink, this bird can fly from Alaska to New Zealand: 11,500 kilometers (7,146 miles).

ALASKA

NEW ZEALAND

OVER TO YOU

If you're interested in testing your limits, don't let aches, lizards, or jellyfish scare you. There are plenty of safe opportunities for kids to prove their skills. For example, IronKids triathlons accept participants as young as three. Just make sure to listen to your body and pay attention to signs of injury and thirst. And most of all, have fun.

Although she didn't race until she was older, Lizzy Hawker was active when she was young too. Instead of catching a bus, she'd walk. Instead of getting a drive, she'd hop on her bike. "Just start!" she says. "Build up slowly and do what you enjoy. The main thing is to do it because you want to."

FAST FACT
Meditation on the Move
Running can be a physical challenge—and also a spiritual journey. As a moving form of meditation, the Sri Chinmoy Self-Transcendence 3,100 Mile Race has participants do 5,649 laps of a course less than a kilometer (half a mile) long in Queens, New York, over 52 days. In the mountains around Kyoto, Japan, monks run for 1,000 days, stopping at shrines and temples along the way.

HEARTS AND HEADS

In addition to slow-twitch fibers and plentiful sweat glands, endurance athletes may have another advantage: bigger hearts. To exercise for so long, their muscles need a large supply of energy-giving blood. Over time, their heart walls may become stronger and their heart chambers larger. This enables their hearts to pump out more blood to fuel their sometimes days-long activities.

They also have special minds. *My feet hurt. I'm tired. I'm bored. I want to sit down.* When you're doing the same tough activity for hours on end, it's hard not to think thoughts like these. Endurance athletes think them too—but, through tons of training and practice, they learn which ones they can safely push past. As Lizzy Hawker says, she feels the pain, does what she can to make it better, and then decides to ignore it.

She also says she enjoys doing things the hard way—which running up and down mountains certainly is. Athletes like her know what they're going up against and welcome the challenge. There's even a state called "runner's high." This is when a runner's brain releases chemicals called endorphins, which give them a sense of joy—no matter how much road lies ahead.

Chapter 5

BODY ⸲ BRAIN BOSSES

The man called Lama Öser has been warned.

… five, four, three, two, one—BANG!

It's like a gun going off near his head, or firecrackers exploding.

Usually a noise like this causes the "startle reflex." When we hear a surprising noise, or see something jarring, the muscles in our faces automatically spasm. Our hearts speed up, our blood pressure increases, and we sweat.

But Lama Öser remains relaxed.

Lama Öser is a Buddhist monk and is highly practiced at meditating. It's the early 2000s and he's visiting the United States for a range of scientific experiments—on him.

With this bang, he shows he's got super abilities. When he hears it while he's doing one method of meditation, in which he keeps his mind open and free of thoughts, his heart, blood pressure, and sweating rise a bit, but his face doesn't move. While doing another method, in which he concentrates hard on one single item, his face twitches the tiniest bit but his body's other responses actually go *down*.

The researchers are astounded.

But what's the big deal? Studies have shown that if a person generally startles in a big way, he or she also tends to strongly feel negative emotions like fear or anger. Startle less, and chances are he or she will have less intense negative emotions too. So maybe Lama Öser has learned to control his not-so-great emotions by focusing his mind.

THE UNBELIEVABLE EFFECTS OF DOING NOTHING

During the series of tests, Lama Öser continued to surprise. For example, he had higher levels of activity in the area of the brain linked with positive emotions. He could more easily recognize facial expressions in other people—which made him more attuned to their feelings. Disagreeable people became calmer after being with him. And all these achievements may be due to his years of meditation.

Meditating is when you focus your mind to become mentally and emotionally calm. People have been doing it for thousands of years. Small carvings from the Indus Valley (now Pakistan and

FAST FACT

Ten-Day Challenge

If you're not used to it, even 15 minutes of meditation can feel like forever—so don't even think of trying Vipassana meditation. Not only do you put aside 10 days to spend most of your awake time meditating, but in your free time, you're not allowed to talk to the people around you or make eye contact. It's an intensive way to learn to accept challenges—like an aching back or feet that have fallen asleep from sitting so long—which will help you deal with challenges in everyday life too.

India) from well over 4,000 years ago seem to show people meditating, and the first written description comes from the same area about 3,000 years ago.

India's Prahlad Jani is also a practitioner. In 2010, when Prahlad was 82, researchers set out to test him, for he claimed he hadn't had a bite to eat or anything to drink since he was a boy—in part thanks to meditation. They watched him for 15 days. They took blood samples. They attached him to machines. He didn't eat or drink, as claimed. Yet his health was excellent. His brain, they said, looked like that of a 25-year-old.

Is meditation magic?

HERE COMES THE ICEMAN

Wim Hof also uses his mind to control his body. Known as "the Iceman," this man from the Netherlands, born in 1959, can withstand all sorts of cold temperatures. He has run marathons barefoot and shirtless—in the Arctic. He has dived under ice at the North Pole. He has been encased in ice cubes, up to his chin, for nearly two hours.

Wim uses a breathing and meditation method similar to a technique called Tummo in Tibetan Buddhism. If you breathe and focus properly, he believes, you can flood your body with oxygen, which will help you keep warm. He also believes you should practice coping with the cold—start by taking a cold shower and gradually increase your exposure over time.

Many researchers have confirmed Wim's remarkable ability to endure cold and are excited about the possibilities. Could Wim's methods help people who work or live in extreme environments stay warm?

Researchers have also confirmed another benefit of Wim's methods: the ability to fight off sickness. Not only can he control his temperature, but he seems to be able to control his immune system, which protects against viruses and bacteria.

As with eating and drinking, though, never expose your body to dangerous conditions. Leave Wim's techniques to him and his trained followers—and put on that jacket!

HOW IT'S DONE!

When a person meditates, their breathing slows down and their heart pumps slower. This means they need less food and water to sustain themselves—but it doesn't explain how people like Prahlad could consume nothing at all.

What researchers *have* continued to figure out are the effects of meditation on the brain. Whether you're constantly practicing your basketball jump shot or memorizing history facts, repeating a behavior over and over changes your brain. Regular meditation does too.

Using magnetic resonance imaging (sort of like a giant camera that can take images of the brain), researchers have been able to peek inside people's heads to see what's going on. By studying people before they learn to meditate and after they've been meditating awhile—and comparing the results with people who don't meditate at all—they've discovered that some parts of meditators' brains get bigger. (See the illustration to learn which parts.)

They've also discovered that long-term meditators have more folds in their brains.

These areas get bigger with regular meditation:

Posterior Cingulate: Active when recalling memories about your life or when your mind wanders; may help you focus your attention.

This area gets smaller with regular meditation:

Amygdala: Involved in fear, stress, and anxiety.

Pons: Produces many of the chemicals that communicate information throughout your brain and body.

This may sound creepy, but it actually means their brains can do things faster, like process information, make decisions, and form memories. And the longer these people have been meditating, the more folds they have.

Temporoparietal Junction: Involved in empathy, compassion, and being able to consider other people's perspectives.

Left Prefrontal Cortex: Linked to positive emotions and highly active in Lama Öser.

Left Hippocampus: Involved in learning, memory, and controlling your emotions.

Also, the electrical impulses called brainwaves—produced when our brain cells communicate with each other—are different. While meditating, both alpha and gamma brainwaves are extra active; these indicate a quiet mind and intensely focused thought.

HAZARD ALERT!

Although Prahlad seemed to have survived without food and water, other people haven't been as successful. An Australian woman named Ellen Greve, known as "Jasmuheen", also claimed she didn't need to eat or drink. But when researchers started watching her during a test in 1999, making sure she had no food or water, her health deteriorated so rapidly they had to stop the test. It was too dangerous to continue. This probably means she *had* been eating and drinking before the test. Not only that, but several other people died when they apparently tried to follow her example.

Without food, our bodies have to use up our fat stores for energy, and then they start to break down our muscles. Eventually, the body is too weak to go on. Without water, our blood volume drops and blood pressure decreases, delivering less oxygen throughout our bodies. Sweating stops, and our bodies can overheat. Our organs eventually fail, and blood vessels can burst in our brains.

The moral of the story: always eat and drink. Although meditation can do great things for you, never take it to extremes.

FAST FACT

Soldier Serenity

The United States military encourages its members to meditate. Before they get deployed, meditation helps them prepare for high-combat situations. And when they come home, it can help them return to their lives by reducing stress and easing chronic pain.

OVER TO YOU

Meditation is such a simple act, and yet researchers have proven it can help with anxiety and depression and reduce blood pressure. It can help us sleep better. It can help us manage pain. It can boost our creativity. It can help us control our emotions and deal with disappointments and surprises in our lives. It can help our brains stay youthful as they age. And for all you students out there, it can help you focus on your schoolwork and get better grades.

Lama Öser says, "This process is within the reach

Think meditation is only for monks? For decades, while overseeing basketball teams like the Chicago Bulls, Los Angeles Lakers, and New York Knicks, Phil Jackson has been encouraging his players to meditate. The regular sessions he leads help them to be more aware of how their minds and bodies interact, to focus on what's happening during the game, and to work as a team.

of anyone who applies himself or herself with enough determination."

While there are many techniques, here's one of the most basic: Sit comfortably. Close your eyes. Focus your attention on your breath.

It sounds easy, but the tricky part is keeping your attention focused. Our minds can be like monkeys, jumping from thought to thought, hardly keeping still. The goal of meditation is to tame that monkey mind; if you find your thoughts wandering, gently pay attention to your breath again. With time and practice, those monkeys will calm down.

Try meditating daily—or as often as you can—for about one minute per year of age. If you're 10 years old, for example, aim for 10 minutes. If you're 11, aim for 11 minutes. It's not too much time to spare for all the improvements it may make in your life—especially if it can help you find peace and balance. Or ace your homework.

COLD COMFORT

Imagine walking outside in winter wearing only a wet sheet. Sounds like a silly, even dangerous, idea.

Now imagine using your mind to control your body temperature. Soon you're so hot that steam is coming from the sheet. The next thing you know, the sheet is dry.

Sounds impossible—unless you're incredibly good at using a technique from Tibetan Buddhism called Tummo, or Inner Fire Meditation.

Science backs this ability up. In one study, researchers discovered that Tibetan monks practicing Tummo were able to raise the temperatures of their fingers and toes. They then studied Tibetan nuns, who could raise the temperatures of their whole bodies, as if they had a slight fever. Finally, they tested people who had never done this type of meditation before; after learning this technique, they too could raise their body temperatures, although not as high as the practiced nuns.

How do Tummo meditators get so hot? First, they use a special breathing technique that produces heat in their bodies. Second, they visualize flames along their spinal cords. Together, these work to raise their body temperature and keep it there.

Chapter 6

DEEP~SEA
MERMAIDS (AND MEN)

The seafloor is rocky and dim, with seaweed and other aquatic plants tucked into crevices. Above, sunlight glitters in a circle on the rippled surface of the water. A long rope snakes from a boat into the depths.

At the other end of the rope, a woman swims along the seafloor, gloved hands reaching into cracks, tucking her finds one by one against her chest. Sea snails, octopuses, sea cucumbers: the woman is collecting edible creatures. If lucky, she'll find an oyster with a pearl. Hands full and feeling the need for air, she rights herself and begins her ascent to the surface.

That's right: this woman doesn't have a supply of oxygen. Although she wears a wet suit and goggles, she isn't a scuba diver with a tank strapped to her back. Instead, dive after dive—slapping only a couple of items at a time into the boat—she's descending on her own power.

This woman is an *ama*, or "sea woman" in Japanese. For thousands of years, generations of *ama* have been collecting food to support themselves and their families, training as teens and then spending up to four hours a day in the water, well into their senior years.

Although they aren't known to be able to hold their breath for huge lengths of time—only a couple of minutes—what is astonishing is how often they do it: up to 150 times a day. No wonder they're known as the "mermaids of Japan."

DIVING DYNAMOS

Despite being land mammals, we humans are actually pretty good at holding our breath—and we do it best when underwater. On land, we generally manage a couple of minutes at most. But in 2009, France's Stéphane Mifsud immersed himself in water and held his breath for 11 minutes and 35 seconds.

By inhaling pure oxygen beforehand—which gives the body more oxygen to rely upon when not breathing—Spain's Aleix Segura Vendrell managed more than twice as long in 2016: 24 minutes and 3.45 seconds. Using the same technique, Brazil's Karoline Meyer managed 18 minutes and 32.59 seconds in 2009.

Freedivers (divers who don't carry breathing equipment) have all sorts of disciplines that test their skills:

FAST FACT
Feeling Blue
Sometimes, little kids get so upset they can't breathe. They turn blue or get super pale, and pass out. The children don't do this on purpose—these breath-holding spells happen automatically. And although they're scary to watch, they're not actually dangerous: once the child passes out, their breathing reflexes kick into action, they start breathing normally again, and all is soon fine.

especially how deep they can dive on one breath. In 2007, Austria's Herbert Nitsch dove 214 meters (702 feet)—about as deep as a 65-story building is high. To do it, he had to hold his breath for 4 minutes and 24 seconds. How did he get that far down that fast? In this discipline, called "no-limits," divers use weights to sink themselves down quickly and then rely on balloons or inflatable vests to zip them back up.

Divers also test how deep they can go on their own power: no fins, no ropes, no weights, no balloons. By simply swimming down and up, New Zealand's William Trubridge was able to descend 102 meters (335 feet) in 2016, which took him 4 minutes and 13 seconds. That's like flipping the Statue of Liberty upside down into the ocean, then swimming from the surface to well below its torch and back—all on one gulp of breath.

PUSHING OUR WATERY LIMITS

How long can humans last without breathing? One former record-holder thinks we'll eventually be able to hold our breath underwater for several hours, and that no-limits divers will be able to descend 1 kilometer (0.62 miles)—over four times deeper than Herbert Nitsch's record. He thinks this will be achieved by using yoga techniques to prep better, or through technological advances in equipment, such as fins made out of more effective materials.

As for our best deep-sea technology right now—and a way to breathe freely while exploring great depths—submarines are the way to go. The deepest a human has traveled underwater in a submarine is to the bottom of the Mariana Trench in the Pacific Ocean: the deepest place on Earth. This voyage has been done twice: first in 1960 by a member of the US Navy and a Swiss oceanographer, and then in 2012 by movie director James Cameron. In two and a half hours, he traveled down nearly 11 kilometers (6.8 miles). In comparison, the world's tallest mountain, Mount Everest, is only 8.8 kilometers, or 5.5 miles.

HOW IT'S DONE!

To survive, our bodies need a constant supply of oxygen, which is why we breathe pretty much nonstop. When we're underwater, though, we can't access the oxygen in the air. Remain without oxygen too long, and the outcome won't be good. So how could Stéphane hold his breath for over 11 minutes?

The key is doing it underwater. When we submerge our faces in liquid, especially cold liquid, three main things automatically happen:

1) Without having to think about it, we stop breathing. Since we don't want to inhale water into our lungs, this is a good thing (for a while).

2) Our hearts slow down. This makes us use the oxygen that's already stored in our bodies more gradually.

3) The blood vessels in relatively unimportant areas of our bodies, like arms and legs, get narrower. This means less blood (and the oxygen it carries) flows into these body parts, and more flows through the parts that really matter, like our brains and hearts.

This reflex, called the "diving response," is

Key aspects of the diving response:

Bradycardia: Our hearts slow down to conserve oxygen.

one of the most powerful ones humans—and all mammals—have. It's how a sperm whale, for example, can hold its breath for about 90 minutes and dive 2 kilometers (1.24 miles) below the surface of the ocean.

People like Stéphane also have another advantage: they train hard. Through

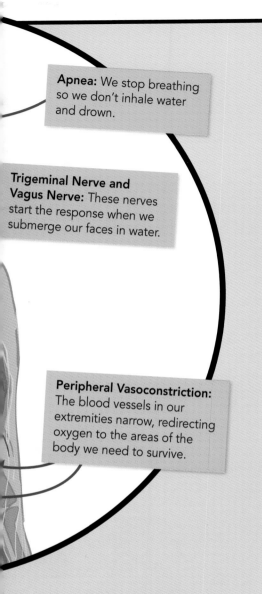

Apnea: We stop breathing so we don't inhale water and drown.

Trigeminal Nerve and Vagus Nerve: These nerves start the response when we submerge our faces in water.

Peripheral Vasoconstriction: The blood vessels in our extremities narrow, redirecting oxygen to the areas of the body we need to survive.

practice, they learn to tolerate the discomfort that comes from holding their breath. They also learn to relax, and a relaxed body uses less oxygen than a tense one. In addition, they may have larger lungs than other people, although researchers aren't sure if they're born with them or if they develop them from the training.

HAZARD ALERT!

It's no surprise there are risks to being underwater—especially when you're holding your breath. If you run out of oxygen, you could black out. If you gulp in water, trying to breathe, you could drown. In 2002, French freediver Audrey Mestre died when her balloon failed to inflate properly. Russia's Natalia Molchanova disappeared in 2015 while teaching freediving—possibly because powerful underwater currents swept her away.

Although it sounds like a good idea, don't prepare to go underwater by gulping in air quickly or taking super-deep breaths. Breathing is a balance between inhaling oxygen and exhaling carbon dioxide. When you hyperventilate, you decrease the amount of carbon dioxide in your blood, but you don't actually increase the amount of oxygen. This makes you feel like you don't need to breathe, but you do. Underwater, this could quickly get you into danger.

And if you ascend from a dive too quickly, the rapid change in water pressure may cause decompression sickness. This mostly happens to divers who use scuba gear and breathe from a tank, but those who hold their breath can sometimes experience it too. Bubbles of nitrogen form in your blood and tissues, blocking the flow of blood. You might get a headache, become dizzy, have a hard time thinking clearly, and feel so much joint pain that it doubles you over. That's why it's sometimes called "the bends." To avoid it, rise slowly and stop for a bit while you're still underwater. This gives your body a chance to flush out the nitrogen before it forms into bubbles.

Holding your breath for too long might also affect your short-term memory, make it harder to pay attention, and harm the neurons in your brain. Although these problems seem to be mild, they can last a long time.

OVER TO YOU

If you're still keen on seeing how long you can hold your breath, don't test it out until you're in your late teens—otherwise, you could harm your developing body. Besides, unlike in many other activities, youth isn't an advantage in freediving. Some of the best have obtained records while in their fifties, and *ama* can keep diving into their nineties.

Being able to hold your breath for several minutes—or being able to hold your breath again and again for shorter periods, like *ama*—takes serious training. Once you're old enough, do it on land before you do it in water. Have a partner at your side to help if something goes wrong. Do it slowly and steadily. If you feel uncomfortable, stop.

While training your body, also focus on your mind. If the idea of being immersed in water unable to take a breath stresses you out, this activity is probably not for you—being stressed means you'll use up oxygen quicker.

And probably don't plan on having a career as an *ama*. The practice is dying out. While there were once many thousands of these sea women in Japan, their numbers are quickly dropping. Not only are there fewer sea snails and other creatures in the waters today, but most young girls aren't interested in taking up diving as a career. One day soon, the mermaids may be extinct.

FAST FACT

That Hotel's a Dive

Humans can hold their breath only for so long, but that doesn't mean we can't stay underwater much longer. Living in an undersea hotel off the coast of Florida, American biology teachers Jessica Fain and Bruce Cantrell stayed underwater for over 10 weeks in 2014.

SHE BREATHES—SHE SCORES!

Good at holding your breath? Why not make a sport of it!

Spearfishing—the act of hunting and capturing fish while underwater and holding your breath—was once done with sharpened sticks. Now, it's done with spearguns in competitions. To see how accurate you are, you can also target-shoot underwater, using weights to anchor yourself to the bottom of the pool and coming up for air between shots.

Or you can take up underwater wrestling, where you try to grab a ribbon attached to your opponent's ankle. Rugby, hockey, and football can also be played underwater—when you need air, a teammate jumps in to take your place.

For extra challenge, add a chill to it. In underwater ice hockey, the bottom surface of a frozen pool or pond becomes an upside-down ice rink. Wearing wet suits to protect against the cold, players enter through a hole cut in the ice, swim in all directions—sideways, right side up, upside down—and use hockey sticks to push a floating puck along the ice, aiming for the other team's goal. They last about 30 seconds before popping up for air.

Chapter 7

SPEED DEMONS

"**B**olt, if you can beat Ricardo in the school sports day race, I'll give you a box lunch."

It's the mid-1990s and eight-year-old Usain Bolt is excited by his teacher's challenge. He knows he's a fast runner, but he's never thought of competing in an official race. While playing in the streets of his Jamaican town, Usain has been able to run faster than all the kids, except his rival, Ricardo. And winning a lunch of chicken, sweet potatoes, rice, and peas—now that's a prize worth fighting for!

On the day of the race, spectators line the running track on the grassy school field. When the teacher shouts "Go!" the competitors take off. As Usain whips his legs and arms back and forth, back and forth, the other racers, including Ricardo, fall farther and farther behind. Soon, Usain is busting across the finishing line.

Years later, the renowned sprinter—winner of eight Olympic gold medals and holder of several world records—looked back on this first race. "I was a champ," he wrote in his autobiography, "and as I tumbled to the ground at the end of the lanes, I knew one thing: being Number One felt pretty good."

CATCH ME IF YOU CAN

Usain's nickname—"Lightning Bolt"—has stuck with him for a reason: no one has caught up to him yet.

His specialty, the short races called sprints, come in many distances, but the 100 meter (328 feet) is the most popular. Because it's short, the sprinters can give it their all—and produce some extraordinary times. In 2009, Usain set the world record in the 100-meter sprint at the World Championships in Berlin, crossing the finish line in 9.58 seconds.

How fast is that? If you count all parts of the race, including getting up from the starting block, he ran at an average of 37.58 kilometers (23.35 miles) per hour. If you take away his initial reaction time and only consider his actual running time, he ran even faster: an average of 38.18 kilometers (23.72 miles) per hour.

And if you look only at his fastest moment, he was running at 44.16 kilometers (27.44 miles) per hour. These numbers mean he was running faster than the speed limit on many neighborhood streets. For a car, that's not very fast. For a human, it's super speed.

As for women, no one has ever come close to the United States' Florence Griffith Joyner. She began running at age 7, was a national track star by age 14, and then set the fastest time for the women's 100-meter race at age 28 in 1988: 10.49 seconds.

AMILEAMINUTEANDNOBREATHINBETWEEN

Our legs aren't our only sources of speed. In the world of baseball, Aroldis Chapman has the fastest arm. Most pitchers can throw a ball at a top speed of about 145 kilometers (90.1 miles) per hour. While playing with the Cincinnati Reds in 2010, Aroldis's ball was clocked at 169.14 kilometers (105.1 miles) per hour. That's way faster than a car zooming down a highway.

People have found other bizarre ways to be fast. There's the most Hula-Hoop rotations in one minute (243) and the fastest time for three people to smash 30 clocks with guitars (31.33 seconds). Other records include tying a shoelace (0.63 seconds) and cutting up 15 portions of fish for dinner (1 minute, 5 seconds).

New York's Fran Capo is the world's fastest-talking woman. She can say 585 words in a minute (9.75 words per second): about four times faster than the average conversation.

Also from New York, "Motormouth" John Moschitta Jr. has been clocked at 583 words per minute (9.72 words per second). In 1995, Canada's Sean Shannon recited Shakespeare—Hamlet's "To be or not to be" speech—in 23.8 seconds. That's 655 words per minute (10.92 words per second).

How can they speak so fast? When researchers studied Fran, they discovered she leaves out pauses between words. She also keeps all her words at one pitch to save time: no raising her voice at the end of a question, for example, or emphasizing important words. Her brain is also slightly different: when she speaks quickly, the Broca's area of her brain, which controls speech, activates more than normal.

HOW IT'S DONE!

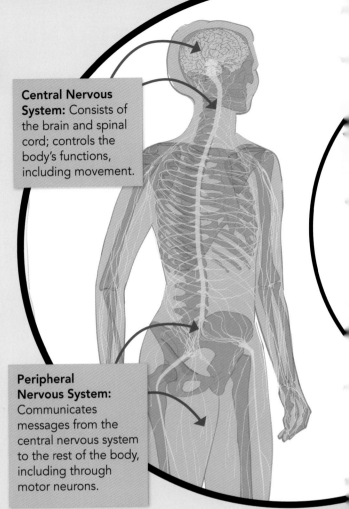

Central Nervous System: Consists of the brain and spinal cord; controls the body's functions, including movement.

Peripheral Nervous System: Communicates messages from the central nervous system to the rest of the body, including through motor neurons.

Sprinters need to access a lot of power quickly, for a very short period of time. They can do this because they have tons of fast-twitch fibers in their leg muscles. There are actually two types of fast-twitch fibers. Sprinters mostly have the super-duper-fast ones that get tired the quickest. And remember those weight lifters? While their muscles are also full of fast-twitch fibers, they mostly have the type that are a wee bit slower.

Although sprinters come in various body sizes, being tall and lean may be a bonus—the longer your legs, the more distance each stride can cover. Serious training is also a must.

In major races, top competitors often finish within a few hundredths of a second of each other. That's faster than you can blink. Sometimes, though, it isn't the running itself that makes the difference between winning and losing. Sometimes it's how fast the runner gets up and gets going.

Frozen in a crouched position, a sprinter has to wait to hear the starting gun fire, and then push off and begin running as quickly as possible. The time between hearing the gun and getting his muscles to move is called the "reaction time." Why can't this happen instantaneously? It's because information has to travel from the ear to the brain, from the brain down the spinal cord, and from the spinal cord to the muscles. This takes a bit of time—for most people, around 0.15 to 0.3 seconds. We're mostly born with the reaction time we've got—there's a physical limit to how fast the information can travel through our bodies—but we can improve it a little bit. For a sprinter, the

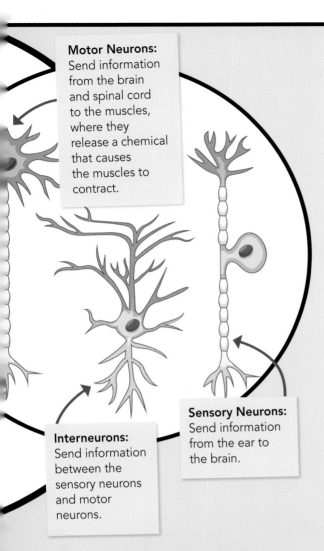

Motor Neurons:
Send information from the brain and spinal cord to the muscles, where they release a chemical that causes the muscles to contract.

Interneurons:
Send information between the sensory neurons and motor neurons.

Sensory Neurons:
Send information from the ear to the brain.

HAZARD ALERT!

Losing a race or being disqualified aren't a sprinter's only worries.

Usain has injured his hamstring, which is one of the most common injuries for sprinters. That's because this behind-the-thigh muscle is used throughout the run and alternates between powerfully contracting and quickly stretching out.

Like all competitors, these athletes also need to stay away from the temptations of performance-enhancing drugs. In the late 1980s, Canadians were hugely proud of sprinter Ben Johnson, who set a 100-meter world record and won an Olympic gold. When he was caught taking steroids, his achievements were taken away.

FAST FACT
She Sells Seashells
Auctioneers are fast talkers, trying to get the highest prices for whatever they're selling, from fine art to cattle. To learn their skills, they may attend auction school, where they practice tongue twisters, breathing, pronunciation, and ways to strengthen their vocal muscles.

best way is to keep practicing by listening for the starting signal and then taking off.

However, a sprinter doesn't want to get going *too* quickly. If she does, she might start moving before hearing the gun. That's considered a false start and could disqualify her from the race.

As with all physical activities, stop if you feel any pain or if you feel you've pushed yourself too far. Take breaks—between exercises and between training days. Even though the goal is to get fast, don't be in a rush. While some people know they're quick when they're young, others don't figure this out until later—which isn't necessarily bad. In fact, sprinters don't get to their maximum speeds until their bodies have matured. Usain, for example, was 22 when he set his most recent 100-meter world record.

Maybe one day, with a little dedication, you'll find a speedster inside you too.

OVER TO YOU

To get speedy safely, learn proper technique. Keep your torso and head upright and faced to the front. Bend your elbows at about 90 degrees, and grip your hands lightly. Keep your arms close to your body as you swing them from your shoulder sockets—and make sure your hands travel from your hip to your lip. Lift your front knee high and straighten your back leg all the way. Start out with short, quick strides, and then make them longer as you gain speed. And remember to also practice reacting to the starting gun.

FAST FACT

Sound versus Sight

When it comes to reaction time, we can respond more quickly to a sound like a starting gun than a visual signal like a traffic light. That's because messages from our ears get sent to our brains faster than they do from our eyes.

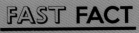

FAST FACT

Daredevils on Snow

Stick a person on skis, plop them on a super-steep slope, and let them go. "Speed skiing" is humanity's fastest non-motorized sport. In 2016, Italy's Ivan Origone clocked over 255 kilometers (158.5 miles) per hour, and his country-mate Valentina Greggio clocked over 247 kilometers (153.5 miles) per hour. If you were driving down a highway, they'd pass you in an instant and be gone.

RACING OVER TIME

Will humans keep getting faster? Or have our bodies hit their limits?

Actually, some researchers think we've gotten *slower*. They found 20,000-year-old fossilized footprints in Australia made by six men chasing prey. By analyzing these prints, they think the men were running about 37.02 kilometers (23 miles) per hour on mud. Yes, that's slower than Usain Bolt's max of 44.16 kilometers (27.44 miles) per hour. But what if these ancient humans had had flat, solid ground, spiked shoes, and years of training? Researchers think they would have beat modern racers.

Researchers also think today's runners won't get much faster. To improve speed, humans need stronger muscles and longer limbs—but these add weight, which slows you down. Sooner or later, the extra speed will match the added slowness and we simply won't be able to run any quicker.

Chapter 8

MATHEMAGICIANS

Eighty dollars for power locks, $195 for power seats, $30 a month for five years for satellite radio, a base price of $320 per month for 60 months. The used car salesman rattles off more than a dozen numbers to explain how much it costs to lease a striped blue van. The potential customer crouches on the ground, head down, eyes shut. He isn't feeling sick: he's concentrating as the figures whiz by: $820 off for his trade-in vehicle, a warranty for $45 a month, an extra $2,830 for taxes. And, just because the salesman likes him, an additional 10 percent discount off the top.

No, the customer doesn't eventually drive off in the van. Instead, this mathematical chaos is being thrown at pretend-customer Mike Byster in 2017 during the FOX TV show *Superhuman*. The goal is to see if math expert Mike can do the calculations, in his head, as fast as he claims. Hearing all these rapid numbers, can he figure out the final price of the van?

"What do you say?" the salesman asks. "Can I get you in this car today?"

Mike stands straight. Without extra time to think, without pen and paper, without a calculator, he says: "Before the discount, it's $26,960. With the discount, we're looking at $24,264."

An assistant reveals the price sticker. Mike is right!

A HEAD FOR NUMBERS

Mike, from the United States, is one of many people who have learned how to do math fast. Another American, Scott Flansburg, calls himself "the Human Calculator." In 15 seconds, he can add a two-digit number to itself 36 times—much faster than someone with a real calculator can do it.

One of the most famous mental calculators of all time is India's Shakuntala Devi. Born in 1929, she was only three years old when she started to show a talent for math. Her father performed with a circus, and Shakuntala began performing too. Soon she had taken over the show.

Before she was a teenager, she was traveling around the world to show off her lightning-fast skills. How fast? In 1977, she was asked to figure out the 23rd root of a 201-digit number. (In other words, what smaller number multiplied by itself 23 times would equal the 201-digit number?) While a computer took 62 seconds to come up with the answer, Shakuntala took only 50.

She proved herself again in 1980. This time, she multiplied two 13-digit numbers in 28 seconds—which included the time it took for her to say the answer out loud.

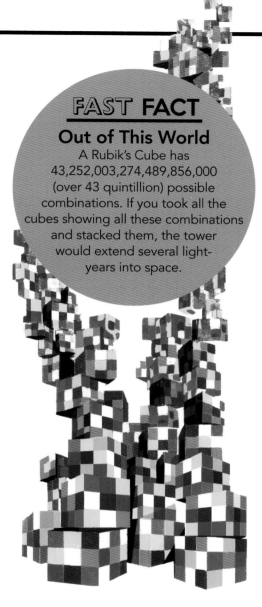

FAST FACT

Out of This World

A Rubik's Cube has 43,252,003,274,489,856,000 (over 43 quintillion) possible combinations. If you took all the cubes showing all these combinations and stacked them, the tower would extend several light-years into space.

Another extraordinary Indian citizen is Priyanshi Somani. In 2010, at age 11, she won the overall title at the Mental Calculation World Cup, which tests mental math skills every two years. In 2012, she became the "mental square root record holder" through the Memoriad World Mental Sports Federation.

IMPOSSIBLY POSSIBLE

Looking for a more frivolous way to demonstrate your smarts? Solve a Rubik's Cube. Invented in the 1970s, this puzzle has become a bestselling toy. With multiple ways to twist the individual cubes and mix up the colors, it seems as if there's no way you can put them back into their original places.

But there is. At the 2017 World Rubik's Cube Championship, America's Max Park solved the puzzle in less than 6 seconds—not quite beating Australia's Feliks Zemdegs's record of 4.73 seconds. Canada's Bill Wang took a slightly different version of the puzzle and solved it in just over two minutes. Not only is that an amazing time, but Bill did it blindfolded!

How can a seemingly impossible puzzle be solved so quickly, sometimes without even looking? Many university math departments have written multiple-page documents that explain the math involved in solving a Rubik's Cube. But unless you're a math whiz, they won't make your cube become less mixed-up.

Feliks has a better idea: learn the how-tos off the Internet. Anyone can do it, he says, by following the simple steps posted online. It just takes practice and patience.

HOW IT'S DONE!

Think of your brain as the workings of an old-fashioned watch. There's a rotating cog, which makes another cog move, which makes the watch hands tick around.

In our brains, doing math is a bit like this. But instead of just one brain part being active, a whole bunch of parts interact and fire into use. First, our brains need to help us read or hear the problem and understand it. Second, we need to figure out how to tackle it. Third, we need to do the math. Fourth, we have to write or say the answer. Each of these steps can rely on multiple areas of the brain—some more involved than others—that work together to accomplish the task.

People who are gifted at math use their brains like this, but the right sides of their brains are more developed and get more use. This may mean they're "seeing" the math problems. Plus, the neurons from the right and left sides of their brains are more interconnected than normal, indicating they're better at exchanging information. Also, the brains of younger math whizzes appear to be more developed than the brains of other children their age and have as much processing power as an adult's—or more.

Inferior Parietal Lobule: Helps us think mathematically and visualize objects; it was bigger than normal in the brain of genius Albert Einstein.

Left Motor Cortex: Shows increased activity while we are writing out an answer.

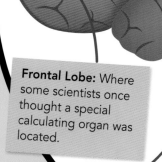

Frontal Lobe: Where some scientists once thought a special calculating organ was located.

Posterior Cingulate Cortex/Frontal Pole: Show increased activity while we are understanding a math problem.

Ventral Visual Stream/Parietal, Prefrontal, and Caudate Regions: Show increased activity while we are working out how to tackle a problem.problem.

Left Hemisphere: Better connected to the right hemisphere in people who are gifted in math.

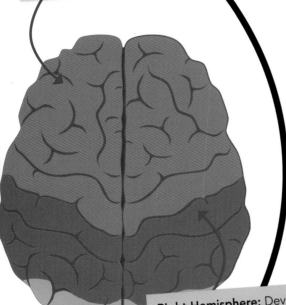

Right Hemisphere: Developed and used more in people who are gifted in math; better connected to the left hemisphere in these people.

HAZARD ALERT!

Although you might get frustrated trying to calculate as quickly as Mike or Shakuntala, there's no risk in trying to improve your math skills. In fact, Scott thinks students should try to use their brains more often, instead of simply memorizing multiplication tables. As a teacher, Mike has toured thousands of classrooms to teach students the tricks that will make them better at math. He says it's like lifting weights: once you get stronger, you can do anything that requires strength.

FAST FACT
A Brainy Weed

Most gardeners know weeds can multiply—but researchers have shown they can also divide. They discovered the weed *Arabidopsis thaliana* can figure out exactly how much of its stored energy it can use overnight so it doesn't run out before it can start photosynthesizing again at dawn. (Amount of starch ÷ number of hours in the night = amount of starch it can use each hour.)

OVER TO YOU

Most of the time, we know how to speak our native language without thinking. To Shakuntala, math was like this: having played with numbers for so long, the calculations were automatic and the answer simply "fell out."

Many mental calculators, though, have specific techniques. Priyanshi, for example, uses what's called a "mental abacus." An abacus is a wooden frame with beads lined up on rods. Slide the beads around and they can help you figure out math problems. Instead of manipulating a physical abacus, Priyanshi visualizes the abacus in her head.

FAST FACT

The Lumps and Bumps on Your Skull

In the 1800s, scientists called phrenologists looked at the structure of the skull to try to determine what was going on with the brain inside. They thought mental calculators were able to perform such amazing feats thanks to a special organ in the front of their brains. This was later proven untrue.

Other mental math whizzes, like Mike and Scott, have learned to use math shortcuts. For example, here's how to square a two-digit number that ends in 5. (Squaring means you multiply that number by itself.)

- 45 x 45

- Step 1: Multiply the first digit (here it's 4) by the next highest digit (4 + 1 = 5): 4 x 5 = 20

- Step 2: Take that answer and put 25 at the end: 20 beside 25 = 2025. That's the answer!

In a study, college students who were taught mental calculation skills were able to improve their mental math capabilities radically. Before they learned the skills, they took an average of 130 seconds to solve a question. After they learned them, they averaged only 30 seconds.

The main requirement for success, though, is a love of numbers. To little-girl Shakuntala, numbers and math were her favorite "toys," and she'd play with them all day long.

Maybe one day, you'll be just as impressive as she was. Until then—quick!—what's 15 x 15?*

*225

FAST FACT

Beastly Sums

Wild animals can do basic math. Frogs can tell different frog species apart by counting the number of pulses in a croak, which helps them know which frogs to mate with. By listening to roars, lions can tell if another pride is bigger or smaller than their own—and then decide whether they should retreat or attack.

PUTTING IT TO USE

Being able to calculate quickly is one thing, but what about applying that mathematical genius to understand the world around us?

The Netherlands' Wim Klein was so good at doing math, he was used as a human computer. In the 1950s, he was hired by a European organization that did scientific research. Electronic computers were rare in those days, so Wim helped his coworker scientists crack the tough calculations.

Another person who used his brain for greater purposes was Albert Einstein. Perhaps you can picture him—an older guy with wild hair. Underneath that big 'do was one of the world's best thinkers, who earned a prestigious Nobel Prize in Physics in 1921.

England's Stephen Hawking was also a physics genius. Not only had he come up with radical new theories—about black holes in outer space, for example—but he also wrote several books that explain these complicated ideas to the average person.

A newer physics genius is the United States' Sabrina Pasterski. Born in 1993, she says she's meant to do physics. "When you're tired, you sleep," she says, "and when you're not, you do physics."

Chapter 9

BRAVE
BALANCERS

Tens of thousands of people gather above the foaming waters of Niagara Falls on June 30, 1859. They mill about while the brass band plays, sit on tiers of seats, picnic on the grass, or pop their heads out of the windows of the trains that have stopped on their tracks for the show.

Then, the Frenchman Jean François Gravelet appears—better known as the "Great Blondin". A hush falls. He steps toward the rope that stretches tiny into the distance, secured on this side of the waterfalls in New York State, and on the other side in Ontario, Canada. He steps onto the rope. Holding a pole horizontally before him, he starts to walk.

Step by step, Blondin leaves the safety of land. Soon, he's hovering high above the churning water. One wrong step, one lean a little too far to the left or the right, and he could plummet to his death. Halfway across, he stops. Does he need to rest? Has he given up? Tightrope walking across the falls is an idiotic idea—everyone knows that.

No. He's pulling a ball of string from his pocket and lowering it to a boat bobbing far below. Someone on the boat ties a bottle to the end. Blondin pulls up the bottle, raises it as a toast to the spectators, and drinks from it—as casually as if he were sitting at a dinner table, not teetering in the air. Stunt done, he calmly continues his death-defying walk.

TIGHTROPE FEVER

Blondin safely made it to the Canadian end of the tightrope that day—and then turned around and balanced his way back to the United States. That was the first time anyone had tightrope walked over Niagara Falls, but not the last. Blondin himself did it several times over a couple of years as his tricks got crazier and crazier: over the middle of the abyss, he would do a headstand on the rope, or a somersault. He walked out on stilts. He carried his manager on his back. He brought out a small stove and cooked an omelet. He crossed blindfolded.

Other people did it too. In 1860, Canada's "Great Farini" (William Hunt) carried out a hand-cranked washing machine and did his laundry mid-walk. In 1876, Italy's Maria Spelterini became the only woman to cross the falls, once with peach baskets strapped to her feet.

Soon, the crowds and mayhem got to be too much. Officials declared no one was allowed to rope-walk over the falls anymore—they wanted the falls to be a peaceful place to visit. That is, until America's Nik Wallenda got permission.

In 2012, 33-year-old Nik became the first person to cross Niagara Falls in over 100 years. He was also the first to be televised while he did it. Because people would be watching him live, the TV network insisted he be tethered to the wire. They didn't want to broadcast a tragedy in case of a slip.

It turns out the safety equipment wasn't needed. In less than half an hour, glistening with moisture from the foaming of the falls, Nik was securely across.

BALANCING THROUGH THE AGES

Showing off balancing skills on a tightrope has been going on a long time, as far back as ancient Greece and Rome. One of the best-known walkers in the late 1700s was Madame Saqui, who performed for Napoleon Bonaparte, the emperor of France.

About 200 years later, France's Philippe Petit didn't perform for the law—he defied the law instead. Illegally, he crossed a wire between the two towers of New York City's World Trade Center. When the police came to arrest him, he lay down far out on the wire so they couldn't reach him until he decided to come in.

Others have stayed midair even longer. In 1993, Florida's Jorge Ojeda-Guzman lived on a tightrope for over 200 days. In 2010, China's Adili Wuxor walked on a tightrope for more than five hours a day for 60 days. This was like walking the length of Lake Superior and back again—and more!

HOW IT'S DONE!

Human bodies are stacks of bones balancing on relatively tiny feet. To stop from tipping over—even on a large, unmoving surface like the floor—our bodies have to constantly adjust. Why can tightrope walkers do this better than most of the rest of us? Researchers don't yet know.

We humans use three systems to tell if we're steady. First, we use our eyes to see how we're oriented in relation to the world around us. If the pictures on the wall are straight, it probably means we are too.

Second, we use sensors in our skin and muscles. Our feet can feel they're on the ground. Our neck muscles know how our head is tilted above our shoulders. Body parts like our joints constantly send information to our brains to tell us what position we're in.

Then there are the specialized balancing systems deep in our ears. Not only do our ears allow us to hear, they also contain three semicircular canals and two organs filled with fluid and tiny hairs (called otolith organs, or "ear stones" in Greek). When we move, the fluid

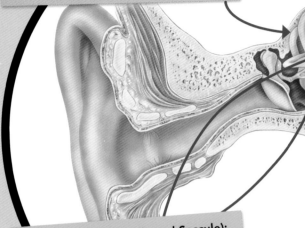

Semicircular Canals: Contain fluid and hairs that detect head movements. There are three canals: two for up and down, and one for turning side to side.

Otolith Organs (Utricle and Saccule): Contain fluid and hairs that detect changes in head tilt and direction, like when you jump off a boulder, rise in an elevator, gather speed in an airplane, or brake in a car.

swooshes around the canals and bends the hairs. When our heads tilt, the hairs in the otolith organs sense gravity. This information goes to our brains and we know what our heads are up to.

If things seem good, we can relax. If not— and especially if we're hovering over thundering falls—our bodies quickly react and hopefully bring us

FAST FACT
Putting the "Fun" in "Funambulist"
Tightrope walkers are also called "funambulists." This word comes from the Latin words *funis* ("rope") and *ambulare* ("to walk").

back into balance.

Holding a pole can help. How? Think of a flower vase. A short, wide vase is harder to tip over than a tall, skinny one, because its weight is closer to the ground and spread over a wider area. The pole lowers and spreads out the walker's weight, making him harder to tip too.

Now think of a figure skater. When a skater wants to spin really fast, she pulls her arms in tight to her chest. The smaller she becomes, the faster she rotates. A walker, on the other hand, *doesn't* want to rotate—that would mean she's falling off. So by spreading out as far as possible by using a pole, she greatly slows any rotation that might happen, giving her more time to correct her position and gain control.

Also, the weight of the pole allows the walker to use his arms, in addition to his legs, to quickly tilt his body back upright when he starts to wobble.

HAZARD ALERT!

Peach baskets, laundry, and a wee-thin wire? These sound like disasters waiting to happen.

Sometimes they are. Nik's family has been performing for generations. They can even create a seven-person pyramid, with someone standing on a chair at the top, all while balancing along the wire—except that one of these pyramids collapsed once, killing two of Nik's relatives and paralyzing a third. His grandfather Karl also died while performing; he lost his balance because of high winds and a badly secured wire.

Still, many tightrope walkers live well into old age. Blondin never used a safety net—he believed that preparing for disaster made it more likely to happen—and did his final performance at age 72. During his 67 years as a tightrope walker, he never got seriously injured.

FAST FACT

Blondin Copycats
Between 1859 and 1896, about a dozen people dared to cross Niagara Falls. Only one died: Canada's Stephen Peer. Although he had done the walk several times, this time, he decided to do it at night after drinking too much alcohol.

OVER TO YOU

To be the best balancer, it doesn't hurt to start when you're super young. Nik started before he was even born, daring the heights while his tightrope-walking mother was pregnant. After practicing his entire childhood, he started performing professionally when he was thirteen. Blondin first performed when he was five.

Start slowly. At first, stick close to the ground—you can follow a line of white tape across the floor, use a long piece of flat wood, or find a circus school that offers a wire just a few inches up. Practice simply standing at first ... then try moving forward while holding on to someone else for support ... then gradually learn to advance on your own. Expect to fall. Lots.

The trick is to keep your weight over the wire. Learn to constantly adjust the positioning of your body. Place your feet one in front of the other. Bend your knees. Look straight ahead to aim your body where you want it to travel, not down where you don't. Stick out your arms or hold that pole.

Most of all, focus your attention. No one's going to keep you on that wire but you, so don't let your mind wander. Keep your thoughts on the task at hand—staying upright. Eventually, you may be able to cross with ease. You may even be good enough to enjoy a tasty omelet while you're at it.

FAST FACT
Without Hard Hats or Harnesses

In 1886, Mohawk men from the First Nations community of Kahnawake, near Montreal, Quebec, were hired to help build a bridge—and proved they weren't afraid of heights. Thanks to their ability to weld steel beams together while balancing high above the ground, Mohawk ironworkers took jobs in New York City and helped construct many of its famous buildings, including the Empire State Building.

TIGHT, WOBBLY, OR WIDE

While tightrope walking means walking across thin ropes or wires, there's also what's called slacklining. Here, the balancer walks across a strip of flat, woven nylon—sometimes hardly above the ground, and sometimes at great heights.

The tricky part, though, is that slacklines jiggle more than wires or ropes do. This extra challenge doesn't stop people from mastering the skill, though. America's Dean Potter, for example, was able to walk a slackline strung between two rock pillars in Yosemite National Park in 2011, plus do his balancing act all the way across Yosemite Falls.

Then there are those who have a much wider base to work with: gymnasts. Some people say the balance beam is the sport's hardest event for women. (Men don't do this event.) While the beam is a whole 10 centimeters (4 inches) wide, it's still mighty skinny for the moves these women manage: staggering flips, handsprings, leaps, and pirouettes.

ACKNOWLEDGMENTS

Thank you to Cornelia Li for her eye-catching illustrations that have helped me bring these amazing stories to life, and to the team at Annick Press, particularly Paula Ayer, Rivka Cranley, Catherine Dorton, Katie Hearn, Danielle Arbour, and Linda Pruessen. Also a big hug to my agent Hilary McMahon at Westwood Creative Artists.

Thumbs-up to all the experts who helped ensure the science in this book is correct: Anthony Bain, Howard Bird, Michael Frank, Fay Horak, Patria Hume, William Kraemer, Matt Laye, Sara Lazar, James McGaugh, Michael O'Boyle, Tom Perkins, Sara Thompson, Kirsten Tillisch, and Paul Zehr. Any mistakes are my own.

And a final nod to the librarians at my local library, who helped me connect with the information I needed.

INDEX

INDEX CONT'D

INDEX CONT'D

SELECTED SOURCES

CHAPTER 1: **MASTERS OF MUSCLE**

Ohl, Paul. *Louis Cyr.* Montréal, Québec: Libre expression, 2013.

CHAPTER 2: **PRETZEL PEOPLE**

Guinness World Records. (2016, April 15). *Incredible contortionist sets backbend record*
[Video file]. Retrieved from https://www.youtube.com/watch?v=7JJw58elFo0.

Richards, Chris. "'World's Bendiest Woman' Russian Contortionist Zlata Twists Herself into
Impossible Poses." *Mirror.* 2013, September 3. Retrieved from https://www.mirror.co.uk/
news/world-news/worlds-bendiest-woman-russian-contortionist-2247803.

CHAPTER 3: **MIND-BOGGLING MEMORIZERS**

"Memory Hackers," YouTube video, 54:01, aired on PBS's *NOVA* in 2016, posted by "Maktaba dz,"
2016, February 21. Retrieved from https://www.youtube.com/watch?v=qyb8Ah3jChw and
http://www.pbs.org/wgbh/nova/body/memory-hackers.html.

"Scientists Study 10-Year-Old Child with Super Memory," YouTube video, 1:32, aired on *60
Minutes*, posted by "60 Minutes," 2014, January 9. Retrieved from https://www.youtube.com/
watch?v=fHnmmb9aaFM.

CHAPTER 4: **ULTRA-LONG EXPERTS**

Barker, Sarah. "A Long Pursuit of Self." *The New York Times.* 2013, April 15. Retrieved from
http://www.nytimes.com/2013/04/16/sports/ultrarunner-competes-on-far-side-of-extreme.html.

Lizzy Hawker website. http://lizzyhawker.com/.

Morris, Sophie. "Lizzy Hawker: What You Can Learn from Britain's Greatest Ultra Marathon
Runner." *Independent.* 2016, January 15. Retrieved from http://www.independent.co.uk/
news/people/profiles/lizzie-hawker-what-you-can-learn-from-britain-s-greatest-ultra-
marathon-runner-a6811201.html.

"The North Face Ultra-Trail Du Mont-Blanc 2012 – UTMB Arrivals," YouTube video, 9:02, posted
by "The North Face Europe," 2012, September 3. Retrieved from https://www.youtube.com/
watch?v=q0ORil5JhXw.

Van Mead, Nick. "Lizzy Hawker: 'I Might Run around 180 Miles in a Week.'" *The Guardian.* 2013,
June 28. Retrieved from https://www.theguardian.com/lifeandstyle/the-running-blog/2013/
jun/28/lizzy-hawker-friday-flyer-interview.

CHAPTER 5: **BODY/BRAIN BOSSES**

Goleman, Daniel. *Destructive Emotions*. New York: Bantam Books, 2003.

"Jasmuheen," YouTube video, 10:48. Aired on *60 Minutes*, posted by "Natasha Koldin," 2010, March 27. Retrieved from https://www.youtube.com/watch?v=cnCuzUd4eC0.

Martino, Joe. "Man Claims He Has Not Eaten or Drunk Any Liquids for 70 Years. Science Examines Him." *Collective Evolution*. 2013, July 4. Retrieved from http://www.collective-evolution.com/2013/07/04/a-man-has-not-eaten-or-drank-any-liquids-for-70-years-science-examines-him.

Wim Hof website. http://www.icemanwimhof.com/.

CHAPTER 6: **DEEP-SEA MERMAIDS (AND MEN)**

International Association for the Development of Apnea website. https://www.aidainternational.org/.

McCurry, Justin. "Ancient Art of Pearl Diving Breathes Its Last." *The Guardian*. 2006, August 24. Retrieved from https://www.theguardian.com/world/2006/aug/24/japan.justinmccurry.

World Underwater Federation website. http://www.cmas.org/.

CHAPTER 7: **SPEED DEMONS**

Bolt, Usain. *Faster Than Lightning: My Story*. Moosic, Pennsylvania: HarperSport, 2013.

"World's Fastest Talking Female," YouTube video, 8:24, Discovery Channel, posted by "SzChristie," 2008, February 8. Retrieved from https://francapo.com/video-voice/.

CHAPTER 8: **MATHEMAGICIANS**

Benjamin, Arthur and Shermer, Michael. *Secrets of Mental Math: The Mathemagician's Guide to Lightning Calculation and Amazing Math Tricks*. New York: Three Rivers Press, 2006.

"BRAINETICS," YouTube video 7:20, aired on ABC's *20/20,* posted by "BraineticsSystem," 2011, July 11. Retrieved from https://www.youtube.com/watch?v=xU7932GWwJg.

Jensen, A. R. "Speed of Information Processing in a Calculating Prodigy." *Intelligence*. 4(3), 259–274. 1990. Abstract available at https://doi:10.1016/0160-2896(90)90019-p.

Kim, Larry. "17 Surprising Facts about Millennial Physics Phenom Sabrina Pasterski." *Inc.* 2016, February 8. Retrieved from https://www.inc.com/larry-kim/17-surprising-facts-about-millennial-physics-phenom-sabrina-pasterski.html.

"Mike Byster Astonishes the Crowd with His Math Skills," YouTube video, 1:59, aired on
    SUPERHUMAN Season 1, posted by "FOX," 2017, January 7. Retrieved from https://www.
    youtube.com/watch?time_continue=3&v=p_098IHOeDI.
Scott Flansburg website. http://www.scottflansburg.com/.
Strachan, Maxwell. "Rubik's Cube Champion on Whether Puzzles and Intelligence Are Linked."
    Huffpost. 2015, July 23. Retrieved from http://www.huffingtonpost.ca/entry/feliks-zemdegs
    rubiks-cube-interview_us_55afe97ce4b08f57d5d35fc6.

CHAPTER 9: **BRAVE BALANCERS**

Anonymous. "An Exciting Scene: M. Blondin's Feat at Niagara Falls." The New York Times. 1859, July 4.
Nik Wallenda website. http://nikwallenda.com/.
Tavares, Matt. Crossing Niagara: The Death-Defying Tightrope Adventures of the Great Blondin.
    Somerville, Massachusetts: Candlewick Press, 2016.

IMAGE CREDITS

All technical diagrams digitally altered by Danielle Arbour.

6 (bottom left, poster) Miscellaneous Items in High Demand collection, Prints and Photographs Division, Library of Congress, LC-USZC4-5122; (top right, Louis Cyr) Unknown photographer / Library and Archives Canada / accession number 1973-211 NPC, item number 3191925; **10** (original diagram) © Alila Medical Media / Shutterstock.com; **14** (Zlata) dpa picture alliance archive / Alamy Stock Photo; **18-19** (original diagram) © Teguh Mujiono / Shutterstock.com; **22** (Jake Hausler) © Richard Shotwell / Invision / AP; **26** (original diagram, inset) © Alila Medical Media / Shutterstock.com; **26-27** (original diagram, main) © Blamb / Shutterstock.com; **30** (Lizzy Hawker) © criben / Shutterstock.com; **34** (original diagrams) © gritsalak karalak / Shutterstock.com; **38** (monks) © Horizonman / Shutterstock.com; **42-43** (original diagram) © joshya / Shutterstock.com; **46** (two *ama*) Pacific Press Service / Alamy Stock Photo; **50-51** (original diagram) © first vector trend / Shutterstock.com; **54** (Usain Bolt) © Petr Toman / Shutterstock.com; **58-59** (original diagram, main) © first vector trend / Shutterstock.com; **59** (original diagram, inset) © Mari-Leaf / Shutterstock.com; **62** (Mike Byster) Courtesy of Mike Byster. Used with permission; **66-67** (original diagrams) © Alila Medical Media / Shutterstock.com; **70** (the Great Blondin) Pictorial Press Ltd / Alamy Stock Photo; **74** (original diagram) © MedicalArtInc / iStockphoto.com.